KNOW THY NUMBER. KNOW THYSELF.

Copyright © 2025 by R.A. Güembes

All rights reserved. No part of this book may be
reproduced, stored in a retrieval system,
or transmitted in any form or by any means—
electronic, mechanical, photocopying,
recording, or otherwise—without the prior written
permission of the publisher.

This book is a creative and educational resource.
It does not constitute medical,
psychological, or legal advice.

ISBN: 978-1-7368151-5-1
Printed in the United States of America
First Edition

Welcome to the World of Numbers

Inside your birthday lives a special number. That number reveals your energy, your gifts, your challenges, and even how you connect with others. Whether you're a kid, teen, or an adult- this book is for you.

Each number gives us clues about our path, our power, and our personality. You'll also find space to draw, reflect, and explore your gifts.

Let's begin!

TABLE OF CONTENTS

Pages

7	How To Find Your Life Path Number
8-31	Life Path Numbers in Detail
32-34	Numbers Working Together
35	Numerology + Emotions Chart
36	Reflection Questions
38-39	Want To Go Deeper?
40	Journal Prompts
41	Your Future Self
42	About the Author
43	Thank you & Stay Connected

How to Find Your Life Path Number

Step 1:
Write down your birthday.

Example:
July 25, 2013 ⇒ 07 / 25 / 2013

Step 2:
Add each part together:
0+7 + 2+5 + 2+0+1+3 = 20

Step 3:
Reduce to a single digit:
2 + 0 = 2 ⇒ This person is a 2.

Exception:
If your number is 11, 22, or 33–don't reduce. Those are Master Numbers!

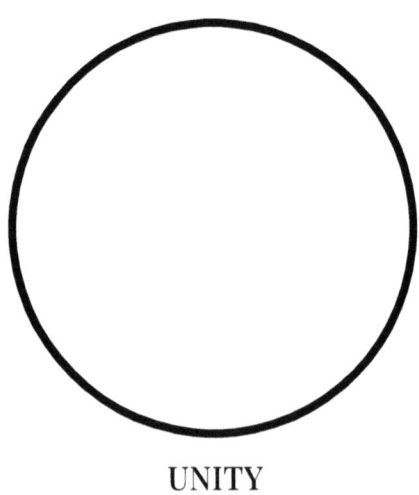

UNITY

THE LEADER

You are bold, independent, and ready to blaze your own trail. You enjoy starting new things and being first.

Strengths: Confident, focused, determined
Challenges: Can be impatient, bossy, or stubborn

Try This: Lead a small group project or plan a game!

Ask Yourself:
- When do I feel the most powerful?
- Do I listen to others when I lead?
- How can I lead with kindness?

Great Careers: Entrepreneur, CEO, Coach, Athlete, Inventor
Famous 1's: Martin Luther King Jr., Tom Hanks, Nikola Tesla

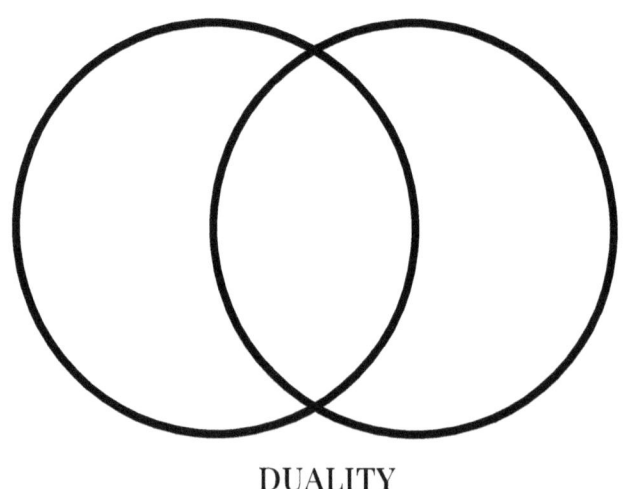

DUALITY

2
THE PEACEMAKER

You are thoughtful, gentle, and tuned into how others feel. You love cooperation and bringing people together.

Strengths: Harmonious, loyal, sensitive
Challenges: Shy, avoids conflict, overly emotional

Try This: Help two friends work through a disagreement.

Ask Yourself:
- What helps me feel peaceful?
- How do I show support?
- Do I express my needs too?

Great Careers: Counselor, Diplomat, Nurse, Artist, Mediator
Famous 2's: Diana Ross, Kobe Bryant, Madonna

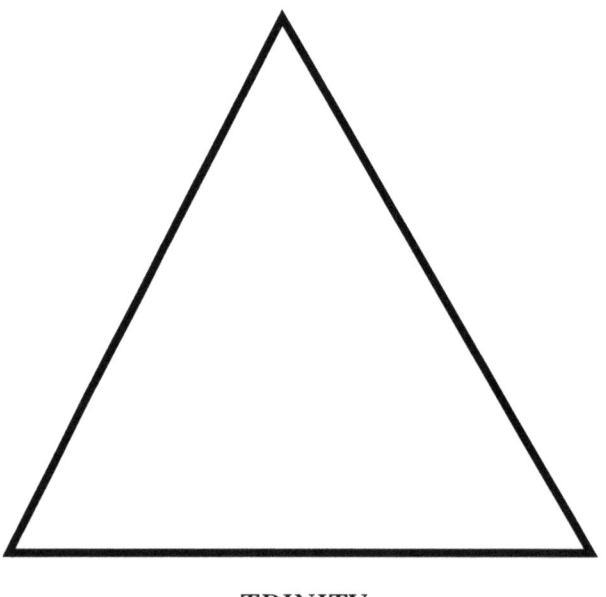

TRINITY

3
THE CREATIVE

You are expressive, joyful, and full of creative energy! You love words, color, and sharing your ideas.

Strengths: Artistic, fun, inspiring
Challenges: Scattered, overly dramatic, sensitive to criticism

Try This: Write a poem or create an art piece about your day.

Ask Yourself:
- What makes me feel free?
- Do I use my voice to uplift?
- How can I focus my energy?

Great Careers: Writer, Performer, Designer, Teacher, Influencer
Famous 3's: David Bowie, Rihanna, Alfred Hitchcock

FOUNDATION

4
THE BUILDER

You are steady, hardworking, and love building strong foundations. You value honesty, planning, and doing things right.

Strengths: Reliable, organized, practical
Challenges: Too rigid, afraid of change, judgmental

Try This: Create a morning routine and follow it for one week.

Ask Yourself:
- What gives me stability?
- How do I respond to change?
- Where can I let go of control a little?

Great Careers: Architect, Engineer, Manager, Tradesperson
Famous 4's: Warren Buffett, Bill Gates, Dalai Lama

THE HUMAN FORM

5

THE EXPLORER

You are adventurous, curious, and always on the move. You love freedom and exploring the unknown.

Strengths: Brave, exciting, quick-minded
Challenges: Impulsive, restless, avoids commitment

Try This: Try something new each day for a week.

Ask Yourself:
- What gives me freedom?
- Do I avoid finishing things?
- How can I bring joy and focus?

Great Careers: Travel Writer, Performer, Marketer, Pilot, Photographer
Famous 5's: Steven Spielberg, Malcolm X, Abraham Lincoln

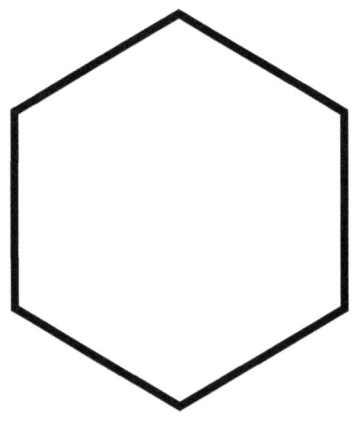

UNION OF OPPOSITES

THE CAREGIVER

You are loving, protective, and feel a deep responsibility for others. You make people feel safe and cared for.

Strengths: Compassionate, generous, supportive
Challenges: Overgiving, perfectionist, controlling

Try This: Write a thank-you note to someone who supports you.

Ask Yourself:
- How do I care for myself?
- What makes me feel appreciated?
- Do I set healthy boundaries?

Great Careers: Teacher, Doctor, Coach, Counselor, Chef
Famous 6's: Eleanor Roosevelt, Michael Jackson, John Lennon

INTERCONNECTEDNESS

THE THINKER

You are deep, reflective, and love exploring big questions. You value truth, solitude, and wisdom.

Strengths: Introspective, analytical, intuitive
Challenges: Withdrawn, skeptical, emotionally guarded

Try This: Spend 10 minutes in quiet, just observing your thoughts.

Ask Yourself:
- What fascinates me?
- Do I share my inner world?
- How do I recharge spiritually?

Great Careers: Scientist, Researcher, Philosopher, Mystic, Coder
Famous 7's: Stephen Hawking, Princess Diana, Johnny Depp

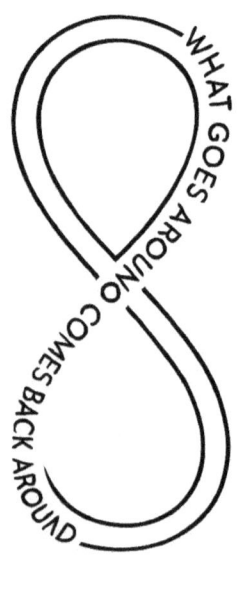

BALANCE

8
THE BOSS

You are driven, strong, and know how to get things done. You like success, structure, and influence. Instant Karma, Good & Bad.

Strengths: Ambitious, strategic, confident
Challenges: Controlling, overly focused on power, workaholic

Try This: Set one big goal and break it into 3 steps.

Ask Yourself:
- What does success mean to me?
- Do I balance work and rest?
- How can I lead with heart?

Great Careers: CEO, Lawyer, Financier, Producer, Public Speaker
Famous 8's: Edgar Cayce, Pablo Picasso, 50 Cent

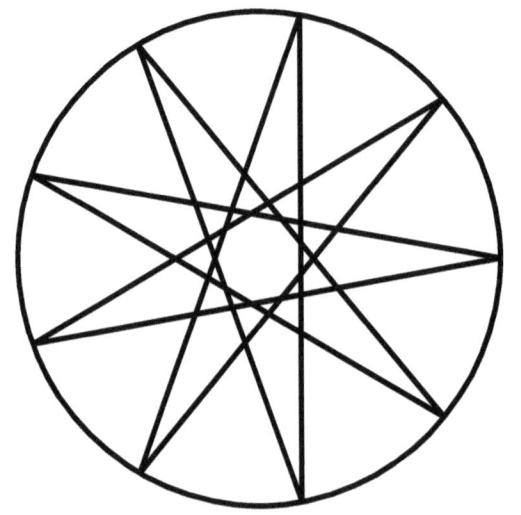

END OF CYCLES. NEW BEGINNINGS.

9
THE GIVER

You are compassionate, wise, and deeply connected to humanity. You want to serve a greater good.

Strengths: Loving, selfless, artistic
Challenges: Overwhelmed, overly emotional, martyr-like

Try This: Volunteer or help a friend without telling anyone.

Ask Yourself:
- How do I express compassion?
- What helps me release pain?
- Where do I need healing?

Great Careers: Artist, Therapist, Healer, Activist, Filmmaker
Famous 9's: Gandhi, Bob Marley, Harrison Ford

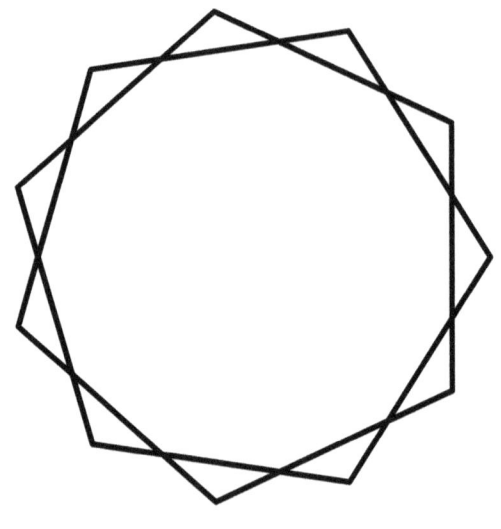

ILLUMINATOR

11
THE VISIONARY

You are intuitive, inspiring, and have a message to share. You feel the energy of the world and want to uplift others.

Strengths: Insightful, spiritual, magnetic
Challenges: Overwhelmed, perfectionist, anxious

Try This: Keep a dream journal and notice patterns

Ask Yourself:
- What message am I here to share?
- How can I stay grounded?
- Do I believe in my light?

Great Careers: Speaker, Counselor, Spiritual Guide, Poet, Innovator
Famous 11's: Edgar Allan Poe, Tony Robbins, Amelia Earhart

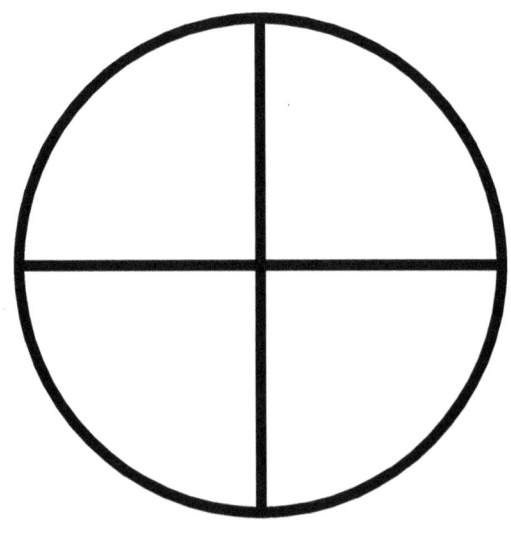

NEW CONSCIOUSNESS

22
The Master Builder

You are both a visionary and a doer. You turn big dreams into real things that help the world.

Strengths: Masterful, driven, dependable
Challenges: Fear of failure, burnout, self-doubt

Try This: Visualize a dream and map out steps to achieve it.

Ask Yourself:
- What am I ready to create?
- How can I stay balanced?
- What impact do I want to leave?

Great Careers: Architect, Leader, Organizer, Philanthropist
Famous 22's: Leonardo da Vinci, Margaret Thatcher, Tina Fey

EVOLUTION

33
THE MASTER TEACHER

You are love in action. You uplift, heal, and teach others through compassion and service.

Strengths: Loving, wise, nurturing
Challenges: Burnout, martyrdom, emotional overload

Try This: Teach something gentle to someone you care about.

Ask Yourself:
- Who do I help just by being me?
- How do I care for myself?
- What's my loving message to the world?

Great Careers: Healer, Coach, Counselor, Parent, Creative Director
Famous 33's: Albert Einstein, Stephen King, Francis Ford Coppola

NUMBERS WORKING TOGETHER

How Your Energy Connects with Others

Every number has its own rhythm. Some like to lead, some love to help, and others dream big or bring the fun. When numbers come together, it's like a symphony—each one bringing its own instrument.

Here's a simple guide to help understand how different numbers can play well together:

The Leaders: 1, 8, 11

They thrive when:
They're respected for their ideas.
Others give them space to shine.

They work best with:

2's and 6's who support with care and calm.

3's and 5's who bring creativity and flexibility.

The Harmonizers: 2, 6, 22

They thrive when:

They feel emotionally safe.

Everyone is working together.

They work best with:

1's and 8's who bring structure and direction.

3's, 9's who bring warmth, expression, and big heart.

The Creatives: 3, 5, 33

They thrive when:

They're free to express themselves.

Things don't feel too rigid.

They work best with:

4's and 6's who bring grounding and balance.

7's and 9's who appreciate the deeper layers.

The Builders: 4, 7

They thrive when:
They have clear plans and purpose.
Others honor their quiet focus.

They work best with:
5's and 3's who keep things fresh.
8's and 1's who bring vision and drive.

The Big Hearts: 9, 33

They thrive when:
They're making a difference.
Others appreciate their compassion.

They work best with:
6's and 2's who share their love of giving.
7's and 4's who help them stay centered.

Numerology + Emotions Chart

Number	Associated Emotions
1	Confidence, Willpower
2	Harmony, Sensitivity
3	Joy, Expression
4	Security, Practicality
5	Freedom, Adventure
6	Love, Responsibility
7	Wisdom, Mystery
8	Power, Achievement
9	Compassion, Completion
11	Insight, Inspiration
22	Mastery, Vision
33	Love, Service

REFLECTION QUESTIONS

Who in your life feels really easy to be around?

What number are they? What number are you?

How can you help each other shine even more?

WANT TO GO DEEPER?

Your Life Path Number is just the beginning.

You can also understand someone's energetic signature more fully by looking at three key numbers:

1. Life Path Number

This is the core of who someone is. It speaks to their soul journey, natural strengths, and lessons in this lifetime.

2. Birthday Number

The day of the month someone was born (1–31) gives a powerful secondary influence.

It reveals hidden talents, inner gifts, and how they show up naturally in the world.

> *Example: Someone born on the 8th may carry a natural drive and leadership presence—even if their Life Path is gentle and sensitive.*

3. First Letter of the Name

The first letter of a person's first name holds vibrational meaning too.

By converting letters into numbers (A = 1, B = 2, ..., I = 9, then J = 1 again), you can discover another layer of someone's personal energy.

> *Example: The name "Luna" starts with an L, which is the 3rd cycle of the alphabet (L = 3). That suggests creative, expressive, and joyful energy.*

Energetic Signature = 1 + 1 + 1

When you combine these three pieces—Life Path + Birthday + Name Start—you start to see the unique rhythm and resonance of a person.

It's not about labels—it's about listening more closely, loving more fully, and honoring how beautifully different we all are.

JOURNAL PROMPTS

What Did You Discover?

1. What number did you connect with most in this book? Why do you think that is?
Write from the heart...

2. Which traits or qualities felt familiar to you? What does this say about who you are becoming?

3. Were there any surprises? New ways to see yourself or others?
How could you use this insight in your daily life?

4. If your number had a message for you, what would it say right now?
Write a note to yourself from your number...

YOUR FUTURE SELF

IMAGINE.

What would your life look like if you fully embraced your number's energy?

Where would you go, what would you do, how would you feel?

Draw it. Describe it. Color it in. This is your vision to keep.

FINAL THOUGHT

We all carry a special frequency. When we listen, learn, and love each other's numbers, life becomes more magical—like a puzzle where every piece fits just right.

About the Author

R.A. Güembes is a creative guide, storyteller, and curious soul with a love for numbers, nature, and the mysteries of human connection. With a background in design and a heart rooted in spiritual exploration, R.A. creates tools and experiences that help people—young and old—find meaning, magic, and self-trust.

His passion for numerology began as a personal journey and grew into a practice of playful discovery and emotional insight. Whether he's building worlds with words or decoding the soul of a number, R.A. believes we all carry wisdom worth sharing.

This book is part of a growing body of work meant to inspire self-awareness, creative thinking, and heart-led living.

www.jolliemedia.com

THANK YOU

Thank you for taking this journey into the world of numbers. Your curiosity lights up the path for others.

Stay Connected

Want more tools, journaling prompts, resources on numerology, sacred geometry or a deeper dive into your numbers?

Contact: whatisyournumberbook@gmail.com

Let's keep learning together.

www.ingramcontent.com/pod-product-compliance
Lightning Source LLC
Chambersburg PA
CBHW040222040426
42333CB00050B/3291